Writing on Your Toes

Writing on Your Toes

poems

Enoch Dillon

Fithian Press, McKinleyville, California, 2012

Copyright © 2012 by Mary McConnell
All rights reserved
Printed in the United States of America

The interior design and the cover design of this book are intended for and limited to the publisher's first print edition of the book and related marketing display purposes. All other use of those designs without the publisher's permission is prohibited.

Published by Fithian Press
A division of Daniel and Daniel, Publishers, Inc.
Post Office Box 2790
McKinleyville, CA 95519
www.danielpublishing.com

Distributed by SCB Distributors (800) 729-6423

LIBRARY OF CONGRESS CATALOGING-IN-PUBLICATION DATA
Dillon, Enoch, (date)
Writing on your toes : poems / by Enoch Dillon.
p. cm.
ISBN 978-1-56474-523-1 (pbk. : alk. paper)
I. Title.
PS3554.I419W75 2011
811'.54--dc23
2011034229

Contents

Homestead

Family / *11*
The Cerberus Dream / *12*
Immigrants: 1911 / *13*
Oregon / *14*
"Now We See Through a Glass Darkly" / *15*
My Mother's Rosary / *16*
Brief New World / *17*
Rodney's Tale / *18*
Intimations of Religiosity from Early Childhood / *20*
The Infatuation Gap / *22*
The Murder in the Larder / *24*

With Wells of Ink

A Fable / *27*
Desk / *28*
Wands / *29*
Ink / *30*
Writing on Your Toes / *32*
The Unauthorized Version / *33*
God Explains Why the Poet Hasn't Been Born Again / *34*
The Trouble with South / *35*
A University / *36*
Not All's Well That Ends MacArthur / *38*
Innocence / *40*
Ireland / *41*
The Cold Warrior Remembers Aunt Irene / *42*

In My Back Yard / *44*
The Milliad / *45*
Mantles / *46*
Webb / *47*
The History of Shoes / *48*
The Murders in the Library / *50*

Destruction of the 20th Century
The Month of the Ground Hog / *53*
Overhead / *54*
Spring Comes to Yosemite / *55*
Washington, D.C.: May 1 / *56*
Dear Friend / *57*
Should Joggers Stop for School Buses / *58*
After the Dog Days / *59*
Portrait / *60*
Indian Summer / *61*
Advent / *62*
Prayer Time / *63*
Parkinsonians / *64*
Politically Correct / *66*
Swan Lake / *68*
The Peripatetic Poet / *69*
Soapy Shakespeare / *70*

To Lighten Up the Night
The Allocation of Scarce Resources / *73*
April / *74*
Rail-Splitter / *75*
For —— Who Carries the Message / *76*
Philosophical Investigations / *78*
Metaphysics / *79*
The Humanists / *80*
Topsoil / *81*

Weeds / *82*
Lampyridae / *84*
Artist / *85*
Open University / *86*
The Atmospherics of Melancholy / *88*
Inamorata / *89*
Cosmos Koan / *90*
First Draft / *91*
Breaking the Cycle / *92*
We Athenians / *93*
1935 / *94*

Homestead

Family

Like a baseball hurler
the surf draws back
curling balls of brine
for mirth-mothers of the land.

Earth dark and lovely
like the African Eve
grandmother of all mothers
and youngsters on the strand.

Whitecaps prove pale
in Easter light
that colors the planet
whether winds toss clouds

or play on sunlit diamonds
where sea gulls, kelp and sand
chalk up Pacific runs,
and your son catches

a green glass ball
that the sea caught bobbing
from a fisherman's net
and lobbed from Asia.

The Cerberus Dream

Wake to Music peals
        opening
"The Great Gate of Kiev"
        rising in pitch to
three glossy dachshunds
        barking me awake

yelping at juncos, squirrels,
joggers, vacuum cleaners—
anyone walking in the garden—
        segueing
to the cool of the day
they whine at God
        sweeping dust from under the rug.

Immigrants: 1911

My mother and eight sisters wearing shirtwaists
all in Sunday white are photographed against
the shadowless but white clapboard farmhouse.

Eleven years a widow wearing black
my grandmother's centered, hallowed by her daughters
returned from church to work in slop and sweat.

They had stolen time for church and photographs
and had to help two brothers in the fields
when Grandfather died fallen from a silo's heights.

Then half the population lived on farms
but soon small farms were not to earn enough
to shelter even one ancestral home.

We are a nation rich with immigrants:
my Dutch grandparents had trekked to Oregon,
felled trees, grubbed stumps, and plowed the deepest loam.

Back East, Italian and Jewish women worked in heights,
in sweatshops where women crippled over sewing machines,
where doors were locked to keep the unions out,

where a fire branded flesh on history,
where one hundred forty-six smothered, burned, or leapt
eight stories from heights of the Triangle Shirtwaist Company.

Oregon

Ocean westerlies rise over mountains,
Rain quenches thirst of farm and forest,
Evergreens flourish under ends of rainbows
Graced like leaping arcs of salmon, while
Owls on sunless sides of cliffs watch
Numen whitewashing with waterfalls.

"Now We See Through a Glass Darkly"

I learned to swim in that black hole
where the silt of Dairy Creek
is buried deep in the Tualatin River.

We dove into that mirror of decay
reflecting that we fancied being men
who braved the mud and snags and chilly rain:

down, down, holding our breath
to out-macho one another
claiming depths we couldn't prove.

One winter the river flooded
across the clover field to our house
then ebbed unearthing clam shells:

just some twentieth-century trash
buried over relics of the Indians,
our shallow assignation with the past.

Our past is shy of many centuries,
and random shards give rise to anecdotes
from superficial glimpses of the deep,

as I had surfaced, gasping to inspire
the crystal of the sky beyond the squalls
that veils an even deeper dark.

My Mother's Rosary

She walked as Oregon mist
grew evergreens and thistles
and whispered for eight decades
to clouds of mysteries
whose firmaments of freshness
like beads from her umbrella
still fell to earth for answers.

Brief New World

A Patriarch with waning power
to rule his present heirs
or promise mistresses a dower
to hush up his affairs

had had himself be duplicated
a patriarchal clone
to see his wishes consummated
through son's testosterone,

but Sonny won't befriend genetics
and joins the bourgeoisie:
now mistresses live like ascetics
and Dad's in therapy.

Rodney's Tale

When Rodney was a little mouse
He read what books he could
And never would be stoned or soused
But practiced livelihood.

Now Rodney snuck in Grandma's larder
Beside the Girl Scout Creams,
Which Grandma hid to make it harder
For Gramps to glut his dreams.

Well, Rodney chewed into a cookie
And had a fatty feast,
So Grandma said to Grandpa, "Looky,
You should help move that beast,

And I will let you eat again
Your favorite dessert.
But don't use traps or any bane.
I don't want Rodney hurt."

But Grandpa set a trap with cheese
Which Rodney wouldn't bite,
Instead some garlic-smelling breeze
Told where he'd been last night.

Then Grandpa baited one more trap
But Rodney stole the cheddar,
For he was just one clever chap
And Grandpa's face got redder.

The trap had never even sprung,
    For Rodney did devote
His time to homework, and his tongue
    Kept quiet as he wrote.

And Grandma said, "Please don't hurt Rodney,
    Just take him out to tea."
But Grandpa often acted oddly
    And baited traps with Brie.

Next morning Grandpa's cheese had vanished
    As also had the trap.
Now Rodney must have been quite famished
To drag that handicap,

For it had sprung on Rodney's tail
    Which was the tiny price
He paid to study, then e-mail
    And warn the other mice.

Intimations of Religiosity from Early Childhood

Within my native town of Goodly Grove
ten thousand souls would worship and implore
some twenty-three discrepant deities.

Priests sermonized me at St. Scrupulous
across Division Street from Bible Lutheran—
both clapboards held uptight by mold and nails.

The other churches, we were told at length,
preached heresy, but Luther was the worst,
a proud, schismatic, and apostate priest—

not only that, was married to a nun.
Such sin was this that when I had to pass
by Bible Lutheran on my way to home

from our parochial school, I dreaded that
its Martin Luther and his wife would lure
me with cleft tongues and pitchfork me to hell.

Years later other churches moved away
to suburb tracts, and so St. Scrupulous
bought Bible Lutheran for a parish hall

while priests and nuns unfrocked and married but
stayed Catholic, choired Lutheran hymns off-key,
and talked of common prayer. The Vatican

had even said that Luther hammered home
some two or three good points, and none took time
to exorcise the demons from the hall.

We Catholics used to make Signs of the Cross
when we were passing Catholic churches, but
I crossed myself by Bible Lutheran

to ward off Satan and today still cross
when passing, knowing that inside the hall
folk-music masses for the overflow

see Catholics worship with no statuary
inside a clapboard chapel that was kept
upright by ninety-five dissenting nails.

The Infatuation Gap

In Memoriam: Douglas "Wrong Way" Corrigan, 1907–1995

We lads grew up in Oregon,
right way until the lasses
told us to fly like Corrigan
or join the working classes.

His plane was tied with baling wire,
Atlantic flight denied.
That he might set New York afire
embargoes were defied.

He aimed for California
by flying to the East—
like cowboys in horse opera
he wouldn't be policed.

He swore his compass went awry,
he'd headed for L.A.
You baby boomers wonder why
and think his flight outré.

We cheered up when we heard the news
for "Wrong Way Corrigan"
had landed near an Irish muse
who heard his orison.

In nineteen thirty-eight the nation
was grounded, unemployed,
and Corrigan's confabulation
could be explained by Freud.

So men whose lives were retrograde
were Doug's apologists,
and Broadway's ticker-tape parade
left women dreaming trysts.

I rue old age in Oregon,
wrong way from younger lasses
who never heard of Corrigan
or lovelorn idle masses.

The Murder in the Larder

Eliza garnished well her grisly plot,
revenge against her fey philandering sot.
By working late he thought he hid affairs
where booze and broads assuaged domestic flares.
He blamed his dalliance on suspicious wife
while Liza sharpened up the butcher knife.
But stabbing's bloody and a woman's bane—
rat poison's easy but too short on pain.
He would pay dearly with some glassy grinds
but even better were sautéed pork rinds.
This perfect murder with no weapon found
the Coroner on fundamental grounds
said gross indulgence broke his Tory heart
in bed excited by a liberal tart.
Eliza was a thousand miles away—
her alibi her tall and dark roué—
she had prepared for months her tit-for-tat
then did him in with saturated fat.

With Wells of Ink

A Fable

A zillion gibbons hit
a zillion typewriter keys
at random
for a zillion years
and duplicated Hamlet:
gibberish,
since Hamlet has no meaning
in a mindless universe.

Desk

That one-room schoolhouse where I dripped
the ink in blobs upon my desk
employed one teacher for eight grades
who didn't have the time to spy
on what bored students read or wrote.
The pen and inkwell left my desk
awash with words, while Rorschach blots
were ghosts relating rustic tales,
for underneath the tabletop
I hid a book of fabled words,
a *Dictionary* out of date
that I then claimed was unabridged.

The dryads who inhabit woods
and fill the trees with sap had hewn
a druid's altar bearing words,
an artifice between the earth
and heaven's fancied polygraph
that said my stories crafted truth
enough for yarns of yesteryear,

and now in floppy disks
my desktop art demythified
lies still to upright monitors.

Wands

Glendower: I can call spirits from the vasty deep.
Hotspur: Why, so can I, or so can any man;
But will they come when you do call for them?
—Shakespeare. Henry IV, Pt. 1, III, 1

Since I discouraged but a token gift
you found a way to show your gratitude:
a pencil from the art museum's store.

I whittle as I did in grammar school
this primal tool to call up metaphor.
I carefully protect the brittle point,

economize the pencil and its words
(I learned that early being poor in crafts
and tools to work the elements of earth)

for I've exhausted all those surface stores
of graphite I've been mining for my tropes
and hope the gods will open deeper caves

where visions, oracles and myths may wait
or my unconscious might deliver dreams
in tides of automatic wonderwords,

and I'd romanticize by saying that
you gave me more than pencil, gave a poem.
But what you gave was ever more that that:

the spirits that you bore from Swansea depths
brought no arcane chants or psychic ghosts,
but language from the deep of centuries

to liven tools like pencils for the craft
that's only learned from other human hands.

Ink

Began when springs
bubbled sunlight
out of the soil

or water
drawn from wells
irrigated dreams

or rain
that soon diverted heavens
into pundit squalls.

The artist's palette
lures lingerie
and rainbows

while novels undress
pastels and flesh
in obsidian ink.

Scribblers spit
inedible ink
for advertising

while the jobless
God writ blue-blooded
are flooded with red.

Ink blots intimate
scented letters
and erotic anecdotes,

as plots with tears
and indigo farces
share white with runes,

words sweating for tenure,
for lampblack lighting
when the lamps flame out.

Writing on Your Toes

When I arise and bend now
my spine cracks like a mirror
and I can't reach down to my shoes.

When young, I could reach but not lace
till thumbs and digits learned to tie—
thereafter, I forgot to think of it.

In Sligo's chilly Hawk's Well theatre
I watched *The Playboy of the Western World*
with characters too poor for shoes.

I said I would have had cold feet,
"Well, you're not wearing gloves:
it's what you've toughened to."

I never learned to knot a tie
so ends would come out even
or scribble barefoot as I must today.

I've yet to leather lumbago:
my grandson laces his shoes with Velcro
and composes on a computer.

The Unauthorized Version

God said to Eve and Adam, "Choose
this lotus-land without the blues,
or opt to live a god-man free
and will to heirs this knowledge-tree
for work and play with ink and paint,
for grace to nurture each a saint."

They opted to inherit earth
and risked that some would censure mirth.
And so it was that man's first sin
was not committed in bare skin,
but dressed with land and wanting more
Cain censored art and started war.

God Explains Why the Poet Hasn't Been Born Again

You prayed I let you win the lottery.
Please note that I have heretofore excused
your bitching, bourbon, and bureaucracy.

I gave you family and fertile muse,
renewed your yellow liver with your soul,
and freed your dogma's grip so you could choose.

Although I've made most blessings nature's role,
you want The Rapture, Lourdes, and Primrose Path
to rescue you and keep you on the dole.

Of course I planted so that your life hath
from time to time some lilies for your lust
but won't enable you to blame my wrath,

for I have given you more tools and trust
than life itself could ever guarantee.
Another god would shake you off like dust.

I've plumb run out of miracles for free
and need a little helping hand from thee.

The Trouble with South

A South excused his loss at bridge this way:
a distant Lord contrived the deck's quartet,
another ruled the way to bid and play
when Chance had shuffled fifty-two coquettes
whose variations last till judgment day.

An absent Guru figured points that scanned
his holdings for the tricks that would suffice,
and though South tries to calculate his hand
such estimates are still too imprecise
to help one lacking sense that cards command.

Impatient South had failed the spade finesse
and blamed his overbid by faulting North,
a partner he himself had chosen for success.
Then West's deceitful diamond king came forth,
and Odds gave East the clubs which South misguessed.

South's victimized by Times in which he dwelt
and picked upon by Fate and Afterthoughts,
yet no one cared the way his heart had felt
when that Last Trump reminded him he'd not
attended to the hand that he was dealt.

A University

is like the Pacific

an ocean
wider than the moon
deeper than the vaults of Zurich
more world-shaking than atomic bombs

an athenaeum
toughened in brine
where channels are dredged
to harbor commerce, peace and curiosity

a studio
whose artists sketch lagoons
and color reefs with varieties of coral

a stage
where winds and waters kiss
and sometimes speak in spindrift and typhoon

a gymnasium
where life once leapt from tidal pools
to consecrate the coastal plains and headlands

an enormous tank
to study tsunamis, squalls and squid

a concert hall
where pipers and surf amuse crustaceans

a ring of volcanic fire

a rocking cradle for fledgling gulls

here and there a hot tub

a school for fishers

a well that rains.

Not All's Well That Ends MacArthur

"Hear tale from veteran lips prove ancient wrong
When base-born Harry banished worthy Douglas,
Son of Arthur, Caesar of the East,
Who would have warred with Mao, barren bard.

With artless Aguinaldo fair deposed
My Douglas led the docile Philippines
Till Tojo seized all tributary realms
Against renowned Douglas—who returned
With islands falling meteors to his feints
Thus saving virgin blood for hearths and fields.

"We trusted Douglas, for the Orient
He understood and honored. His genius
Did pacify rebellious provinces
Till that ambitious Dean of Acheson
Misspoke and treacherous Kim invaded South.

"Bold Douglas, knowing the habiliments
Of Oriental minds, outflanked the brute
And marched apace to Yalu's bloody banks—
He trusted fortune, not that Harry rogue,
Nay roguery marvels more than Harry had:
Say politician Harry, and his deed,
A punch of little Harry to the Right.

"My chronicle reputes my General who
Would have but plucked his crumpled hat and pipe
And all his honor just to ransom lands
For Western husbandry. He knew the East's
Affection for the West. But villainy!

"My Douglas's charisma lost, besmeared
Forever on the Yalu's cursed banks—
Dark spectacles arose from fiendish deep
In China's nether land. Now that was plot
Disgracing Douglas who did trust the East
To keep its place.

                                        "Now fair sit winds for Nam,
And Hark! the William of Westmoreland comes
Bearing Lyndon's rapt encomiums."

Innocence

Korea, 1952

I suppose recruiter's quota
inducted Private Dun Smith
from his heartland swamp
of Bibles, guns and snakes.

He fared by animal survival
and backwoods bromides,
still I remember his Christian
prophylaxis: "I've drunk
water from a creek
that ran over a dead gook,"

and when we ran the whores
out of the combat zone, Smith's
crying, "But she was clean,
Lieutenant." Later standing

upright he caught a chunk
of Chinese shrapnel in the chest.
I suspect he would have said
"It had my number on it."

Ireland

Isle of umbrellas
rhododendron jungles
and wells of ink:
the Gulf Stream greens the sunlight
as God opens palms.

The Cold Warrior Remembers Aunt Irene

1929 Blond Irene was seldom mentioned in our Catholic home.
She married a Doctor and honeymooned in Old Vienna,
soon divorced and fled to Los Angeles: happy, she said.

My Kiddy Account cashed two cents on the dollar:
we couldn't afford the Marines in Nicaragua,
and even Doctors couldn't support a wife plus mistresses.

But ecstasy grew orange in the land of the swallows
red tiles and gossip. Gorged on the then clean air
Auntie shouting *hallelujah* was baptized in the ocean.

1944 Drafted at eighteen from books and depression
I awakened somewhere in desert California
staging for the Philippines where I expected to die.

Before I died I toured the city of celluloid dreams
with an Aunt two years older than mother.
We whirled from bar to beach and beach to bar.

In a bar off Pico hidden from God and Sunday sun
I heard men snicker, "---young." Aunt grabbed
this youngster's hand, "Let's get out of here."

1967 While Johnson rioted in the halls of the White House
and the Howard Hughes Penthouse was shrouded in smog
I haggled with merchants of death before seeing Irene.

In her dark bedroom on Soma she passed in and out
smelling of stale beer. Now only her face yellow—
bloated, sweating, sniffling—she said, "Kiss me."

I poured a stiff drink first and looked away
at her trunk still carrying its sticker from Vienna,
an altar iconed with photos of laughs and memory,

still storied despite a generation of cigarette tars—
with her Doctor, with my father in AEF olive,
and with a young soldier at the Douglas plant:

a buxom Irene shaped in Hollywood slacks. And suddenly
I saw what the men in the bar had been talking about.

In My Back Yard

News Item: WWI Poison Gas Weapons Buried Under Washington's Once Exclusive Spring Valley

Once fallen poets puffed this real estate
of priceless manors and magnolias
for lobbyists, vice presidents, and heirs.

But recent digs for new colonials
unearthed artillery shells and arsenic
and later mustard gas and lewisite.

Spring Valley? Did not the brass hats know
munitions junkyards just like garbage dumps
had best inherit wastelands of the earth

and better stashed near Appalachian meek,
not this spring-green estate where covenants
once shrouded lily-white suburban growth?

A Major-General's not made three stars:
claimed arsenals soon free of poison gas
but can't clear tennis courts of arsenic.

If even bards who had agreed to shill
recanted when the cover-up had failed,
such better living over chemistry

won't help the meek and even heirs survive
today's pollutants and atomic plagues
metastasizing for thirty thousand years.

It is nineteen nineteen—I see fresh dirt
near winter fires where sheds are being burned—
the sign "Death Valley" has already blistered.

The Milliad

An Irish copyist circa 999

In ages after Sun was lit
and God had fashioned men with wit,
some chose to be so gullible
they swallowed ancient chronicles

and failed to investigate
millennium's initial date,
the time that Holy Jesus born
beneath a star in Capricorn.

Now Magi saw His star appear
when Herod was alive to hear,
and Rome's historians agree
that Herod died in four B.C.

And though millennium has passed
no hell-fire torched the orgiast,
no Rapture rescued all the chaste,
few lords reformed below the waist.

Yet I suspect that some divine
will still contend it's God's design
to censure women's puckered lips
and usher in apocalypse,

so let us skeptics also pray
that Jesus spare the world today,
its prophets, gulls and heretics,
and kibitzers from Bishoprics.

Mantles

This layered hospice—

with ozone thinning
to cancer skin,

shelters shrouded
by Chernobyls
and oil scum,

an inch of humus
flayed by floods
dust devils and finance,

tropic forests
slashed and burned
for gold and ranches,

and ocean currents
irradiated
by submarines—

hugs here and there
Samaritans'
green comforters.

Webb

When wires and waves outnumbered houseplant vines
his wife decoupled from his cyber-shrine
where sectors were surveyed with camera,
sound sensors and alarmed insomnia,
along with newer programs for computers
to help defend against his persecutors.
No longer does he see a human bare,
pornography's his Internet affair:
outside the world's a wasteland anyway
confirmed in televised communiqués
and nature's losing in the competition
now that most nerves and cells are air-conditioned.
He has been joined by millions of like mind
erecting fortresses but unaligned
who fear that others wasting kilowatts
will trigger blackouts. What hath God now wrought?
Then shouldering more chips with derring-do
he took to drink and all his circuits blew.

The History of Shoes

—in the Twentieth Century

Our century began with gents in spats
when ladies never would be seen in flats
and wrappings shoe the jobless Democrats.

The Great Depression was awash with news
of people hoarding cardboard that they'd use
to cover holes in their one pair of shoes.

When summer sports were played in weedy places
your dime bought worn-out sneakers for the races
you loosely ran because of knots in laces.

The Army issued men their boots and braid
to show off spit and polish on parade
for which they'll have no need when they invade.

Dance chaperones were warned that girls' selections
of shiny patent leather brought reflections
which gave the boys inopportune erections.

Then Adlai's shoes were splayed upon his desk
with holes some voters thought weren't picaresque:
a Brahmin posing poor deserved burlesque.

Those beatniks, hippies and drug-addled vandals
who covered up the smell of pot with candles
were travesties of Jesus wearing sandals.

Imelda bought her thousands in poor style
and Khruschev banged his shoe so juvenile
while poorer poachers skinned the crocodile.

High heels and spikes may give a lift to grumps,
those men who need to ogle wriggling rumps
but women said, "we'll take to wearing pumps."

Then came the days of joggers and bold streakers
when grungy youths and even banquet speakers
shelled out two hundred bucks a pair for sneakers.

The Murders in the Library

When our budgets were cut
the unkindliest whacks
were machetes that swung
at all library stacks.

The first folio hacked
was *Das Kapital* Marx,
an economy death
for his turgid remarks,

which nobody read
so none ever complained
till the censors did in
Willie Yeats' *Crazy Jane*.

Soon Jane Austen was slashed
and all ironists bled—
Nora's novelist James
snuffed in Molly Bloom's bed.

Blokes commissared Blake
and The Bible's life ceased
for its writing of plowshares
and a pruning-hook peace.

And they buried the bodies
in secret Swiss vaults,
perfecting their murders
with atomic assaults.

Destruction of the 20th Century

The Month of the Ground Hog

Faulting a wimpy mascot
February thaws in overheated malls and basketball.

The sun's prophetically correct
to glitter earlier each day on concrete canyons.

"February" will not scan with ease
and thus red-lined from doggerel for valentines.

It heralds presidents as heroes
whitewashing shadows from recessions and revisionists.

Gophers grub in high-rise caves
until they masquerade with glitz on Fatty Tuesday

wherefore Holy Lent begins hung-over
with promises to fill poor-boxes with the price of booze.

On election years a day is added
to jostle lunatic cycles, digital clocks and Pisces

as the planet tilts toward winds,
and waves of light lure lemmings, mad to hug the greens.

Overhead

If you love hats, see Paris in those days
when April breezes played upon berets—
you're in the nineteen twenties acting gauche
by ogling women in a toque or cloche

or cover up your head with black sombrero
from Mexico to Rio de Janeiro
where beauty still parades in white mantillas
delighting even despots and guerillas.

But JFK scorned hats as wimpish frills
and Jackie's shriveled to a box for pills—
gone soon were Easter bonnets and chapeaux
(like sonnets deconstructed into prose),

gone even from the nuns were veils and wimples
that warily accented eyes and dimples,
gone trilbies, derbies, Bretons, tams, and boaters
and gone the best caparison promoters—

we cannot count the loss of alchemy
that covered bald and maned in mystery—
now all investments fade to plain or pap
save poets wearing worker's scarf or cap.

Spring Comes to Yosemite

Here granite cliffs still scan like sentinels
as forests nurse a million metaphors
with thaws that soften tempers of rebirth
till glaciers, thunder squalls and tremors limn
new tempos for the runes of waterfalls.

Washington, D.C.: May 1

Here understatement stalls
upstaged by pothole threats
while April sleet and squalls
abruptly turn to sweat.

Our fronts come lightning-staffed
like spikes are polygraphed

to tell us Spring's a lie,
yet fancy, seldom hushed,
soft-blooms as sunlight spies
azaleas, white and blushed.

Dear Friend

This August with the dog-day's end
the twilight moon is smoky gold
obscured in part as maple leaves
draw silhouettes of harlequins.

In Europe it is Matins now.
The same Atlantic moon in silver
tops the steeple of the night.
From pratfall dreams you bounce right back

to fancy sultry nights as farce.
Your letters say the limelight moon
will purge fatigue with lunacy,
forgive no star that's serious.

Should Joggers Stop for School Buses

When autumn leaves and youths show off and swap
date gossip at the Third and Lincoln stop,
when baby boomers once omnipotent
have now matured into establishment,
then joggers junk their brogues for canvas shoes
to sweat last night's excess of talk and booze
with grimace, grunts and grit to keep their grip
upon their cohort's claimed one-upmanship
and later in the sauna talk computers
for each is smarter than Bill Gates' tutors,
and when aerobics prep such muscle bound
to think they lead the youthful merry-go-round
and dream they're lusty boys stilled bussed to school
excited by the lads from Liverpool,
you'll see the winded joggers come abreast
as girls continue gossip, unimpressed,
though some will giggle at the sweat that pours
from men who lumber like the dinosaurs
up to red signs against the proposition
they're leaders in correctness and coition.

After the Dog Days

That golden coracle which tacked
upon the Stonehenge solstice
has for two months now

curved down toward southern skies
and soon ancestral isles will chill
in autumn of our northern calendar.

As darkness stretches out the night,
my own belief in cycles shaken,
I fear you've vanished south forever,

yet Newgrange oracles had left
a chink in lapping stones to light
the promise of our winter solstice

that solar spindrift will come round
to conjure crocus out of loam,
and so you write at August's end

that augurs of the sun's return
now gild your Austral winter.

Portrait

When fireflies had trimmed their beacons
sunlight, wandering south with easel,
summoned autumn from its cranny
to coat our naked memories
against a galaxy of ice.

Indian Summer

A stranger's sun
enchants from chill,
the cosmos fallow.

Leaves, gold and rouge,
will lure to bed
the frosty squirrels.

A fireplace charm
would gather all
around the apples

like Eden's fall
some billions past
of all the hallows

when God struck flint
to warm and fill
a world of kinfolk.

Advent

Late Fall composting its colors
muffles the prophet who flushes
graveyards with a squall of squirrels
                        to store the wilting sun.

Space dwindles, eaten by moths,
to frost a million million stars
girt by the emptiness of God
                        whose demands of late

have left black holes of solstice doubts,
and yet perchance an answer too,
for we've struck flint and fired the hearth
                        smelling of fresh soap.

Prayer Time

If walks from markets seem too chaste a chore
to value even on these vernal days,
if all my fancies hasten to deplore
such distances that multiply delays,
may I yet learn to smile like Socrates
and wander past the meretricious malls
to listen for the hushed epiphanies
in instants cupped from cosmic waterfalls.

I'd seldom find the time to meditate
but for the ticket queues in wonderlands,
and though my reveries still titillate
with country fairs, saloons and ocean strands,
may walks from all this bounty be my muse
and fill the nothingness my wants would choose.

Parkinsonians

We shuffle, shake, and slur as if we're drunk
and hunching over find that we have shrunk.
We give instructions to once nimble fingers
and wait awhile as our brain malingers.
We cannot bend or reach to tie our shoes—
our faces freeze in constipation blues.

We dress while drooling tiny waterfalls
from heads that jut out like Neanderthals
whose guilty ego often urges hurry
so we will fumble buttoning with worry,
for we will be embarrassed when our host
will have to help us cut our dinner roast.

It may be poisons from deep-water wells
led throats to low and lower decibels—
now treatable with pills that are emetic
our tremors might be also found genetic,
but fifty years ago our stance was green
when we began to lose our dopamine.

We practice what we can of smiling strides
and stand upright, self-pity's suicide—
and if our writing can't be helped by tutor
we try composing on our son's computer.
Remember that it's our own soul we curse
when frowns and quits anticipate the hearse:

Instead we thank our God we're somewhat spry
to exercise despite our alibi
in hope that reason in us older farces
will keep our aching muscles off their arses—
for now let palsy swing with levity
and daily mine our mind's epiphany.

Politically Correct

"You not only slouch, you're listing to the right."
—The Poet's Neurologist.

A famous pop psychologist
will pigeonhole a fright
to soothe the Tory who'd been kissed
for listing to the right.

One Lefty is a plagiarist
of language mainly trite,
a novelist necrologist
who's listed *sybarite.*

Political economists
survey the plebiscite:
statistics prove that they had missed
a listing to the right.

An academic socialist
says Marx has died from blight,
to get a grant this strategist
cites lists of socialites.

Two Tory bred misogynists
are overly polite
when naming sociologists
blacklisted by the right.

When many try to coexist
they're labeled parasites:
among those hung, an ironist
died twisting to the right.

Now would you ever want a tryst
with Lefty who's not quite
a bleeding heart apologist
who listed to the right?

Swan Lake

Old Europe's forests whispering stories
to this whirling globe of skyscraper cities,
I love New York, I love New York.

Mist clears to a moonlit lake near oaken roots—
under a hanging cedar swans uncurl maidens
in an eddy to tutus from twilight till dawn

when Rothbart, a pork-barrel posing as an owl,
will alchemize idealist flesh to feathers
and Siegfried's tutor drink Romanticism.

Siegfried and Odile's feet forget the earth
in front of a mirror where smoke enshrouds
intrigues in brownstones and city halls

while Rothbart seals the pre-marital contract
conjuring the true Odette into the mirror—
to civic horror the wrong politician's in bed.

Siegfried and Odette leap into the orchestra pit,
form earthly coalitions instead of drowning,
escape a pas de deux to *liebestod*

to stage pirouettes of power struggles,
spectator politics, and smoke and mirrors.
(The tutor who made up this tale staggered to the polls.)

The Peripatetic Poet

Jogging to out-race Atlantic's dawn
and catch the moon three quarters spent,
          has slackened suddenly
                              and can't recall
if isles christened *Langerhans*
enrich the

          Sea of Tranquility

                    Gulf

                         or Blood Stream.

But what did it matter?
Loping further west where memory's
reborn with second wind
he leaps to undiscovered isles
where
he smarts from spindrift,
hears surf lapping in new fonts,
and sees the moonlight walk
on whitecaps of Pacific brine.

Soapy Shakespeare

Now follow this: Will loves a nobleman
but urges him to wed and make an heir,
while Will will lie with sonnets he began
because his own dark lady's left him there.
But when she's caught with clothes and hair all mussed
still lying in the noble's youthful bed,
poor Will is left with his vicarious lust
as both his partners cheat on him instead.
To reassure his sonnets' subsidy
Will writes the most to win his patron's prize
reserving for his wench some flattery
when he day-dreams it's Will with whom she lies:
so Will composes sonnets that are gay
with lies about which love he'd rather lay.

To Lighten Up the Night

The Allocation of Scarce Resources

Some fifteen billion years ago
God lit a firecracker
that exploded in Its hand,

big bang of quarks and radiation
which mutated into molecules
and dinosaurs and sour moods.

I whimpered to my bankrupt God
why not create a solvent universe,
and He said *that's your job.*

Well I can handle supernovas
quasars and the nebulae, but not
black holes of debt that suck.

She answered *do you want eternity*
that's stuck in youth of itch and angst?
If, instead, you chance my murky way

I will tax you for your deficits
but, for potholes of self-pity,
will ration you the levity of angels.

April

"God renews the world in every instant."
—Ruysbroek

Arthritic Maples arch to gravid green

azaleas coexist with mud and thistle

cherry blossoms drift to whitewash
potholes, dandelions and joggers

dogwoods are arrayed for opening night

the morning's planetary showers
foreshadow noon's éclat of palettes

thunder hardens walnut, oak and pine
for sawmills whirring near the garden

squalls freshen roses for a reverie

shoots gossip in the skinny loam

earth girds to carpenter and landscape
neighborhood for barrio and suburb

life is given its billionth second-chance.

Rail-Splitter

I've often split
a lawyer's hair
for senators

a block of wood
to kindle fires
beneath the idle

and shrinking split
disappointment
from depression.

I've even stooped
to crudely split
infinitives

but only God
has dared to split infinity.

For —— Who Carries the Message

"He listens well who takes notes"
—Dante

Your whiskey voice escaped from oaken woods
to pray at twilight's mass behind my pew.
We said the "Our Father," then we turned
to touch each other with that sign of peace,
I've dubbed *the love thy neighbor ritual—*
young hands thus graced the liver spots in mine.

October ended when the trees had flamed
out gaudily, a moment just before
the rains had stripped them all to nudity
and paralyzed November's moods in mud.
I can't believe God listens to my prayers
and I would doubt the sanity of One
who'd waste his capital on my requests,
for I believe that all creation was
so fitted, fed and forged from archetype
its operation needs no miracles,
its no-fault flaws just part of God's design.

Must I believe God spoke through Dickinson
or sculpted the *Burghers* for Rodin, or sang
life's joy in Beethoven—must I believe
the wolves who whistled for your hugs were tamed
because you sent Saint Francis' words to God?
Could I believe that God's at all concerned
that you or I deserve a parking place?

Although my brooding eased since our first prayer,
such healing comes from nature's goads, not God
whose delegations aren't revocable.
So when I say I pray for you I mean
I ask St. Francis fashion me as meek,
not to inherit earth but earn that hearth
where God himself had kindled you and me.
To ask and wait is nature's way we grow
when patience warms a bit of universe
and compound interest works miracles.

I think God's spirit hides within our flesh
where more than galaxies await new words
to multiply his sparks of love within—
your fire has lightened up my prayer and you
became yourself a prayer's enlightenment for me.

But then, you ask, *if God can start all that,*
might not she answer even petty pleas?
Was not such scope for us a miracle?
Would God withhold the power given you
for miracles deny it to herself?

Philosophical Investigations

If most of this universe is dark
to our eyes and instruments
across what interstellar void

will quasars, dwarfs and emptiness
discover our naked souls
and their history of silent films?

When we lighten up with rainbows,
the Big Bang's crazy-quilt,
and multi-splendored diversity,

do we ever pause a moment
to see more than ashes, mud and rust,
and wonder if we can ever see

how a universe took quarks and quibbles
from a blinding burst of fire and kindled
a field of sunflowers?

Metaphysics

I've read and just put down John Donne
like Shakespeare's mistress' breasts, said *dun,*
while Yeats's Maude was surnamed Gonne,
though donned with gun, pronounced like *gone.*
An autocrat who was not hung
or drawn and quartered after dawn
said Deng is dead but is not dung
instead a red automaton
to whom the gods were ever none.
Donne could have been an Oxford don
or monk called dom, but lover John
whose metaphors were highly strung
found wit conceitedly belonged
to wooing, sonnets, evensong.
So sing your wife and God in tongues
(for love is *ding an sich,* not dung)
thus: Shakespeare's mistress, monks, John Donne,
and Yeats along with Maude, his swan,
those Oxford dons, and even Deng,
although done in are never gone.

The Humanists

From Stonehenge to digital watches
measures an overnight florescence
in the teen-age of the cosmos

when God and the angels and algae
have humbled themselves as consorts
to help us transform outside the crypt,

and happy too for our visit,
their lives dull and hermetic
in a universe of stellar dust.

Topsoil

When standing on my head I see
the stars as if they're roots
for green-leafed orchards, grins and words,

believe I stand on cirrus isles
within a lake of blue,
my head akin to risen apples.

I see the waterfall as if a fountain
while sea gulls freed from doubts
fly patterns underneath my feet

where they soar upside down near kites
that somersault above
the loam of life's galactic dust.

And sometimes when the rains obscure
the world below my feet,
my eyes look in the green for light:

my head still touches grain and graphite
as I imagine walking on the wind
and drawing ink of cosmic wells

near unseen roots that claw the sky
and wonder how life's nourished
from the other side of the farthest stars.

Weeds

Elbow crops
fuel forest tinder
crack concrete.

Somewhere they
color roadsides
with thistles, foxfire
and rhododendrons,
prolific belles
for slash and burn

like Amazon jungles'
uncounted species
wasted for beef and gold.

When dandelions
glut our greens
will their paratroopers

forgive us
for thinking ubiquity
cheapens beauty?

Wild flowers
wild nights
wild stars

at random?

Clover thought weed
renews the earth
and lends its luck:

what if wildings
further evolution
unriddle creation

once a mother
took her son afield
and named the flowers?

Lampyridae

Once fireflies that leapt from galaxies
to rise anew from lake azaleas
had flickered brighter as the darkness fell
and rode the twilight like a Ferris wheel.
Then young we caught and jarred some lightning bugs
to live forever in tomorrow's sun
whose limelights glared so bright our insect eyes
forgot that time had only stayed July.
And now light-years away your face has dimmed
yet glow-burns candle-lit as Vespers prayers
ask lambent constellations on the lake
be rendered words by wands of ink so that
we foolish wights no less than galaxies
may trim our lamps to lighten up the night.

Artist

circa 1963, Dublin

If this moth-eroded sweater
no longer fetters the cold
observe it from a distance

those now faulty geometries
blur to persistent liturgy
of woolen-witched infinities

come close to see preserved
that stitch of provenance
"The Needle of ________ _____."

Open University

"Error of opinion may be tolerated
where reason is left free to combat it."
—Thomas Jefferson, Librarian

Inside the new moon
in twilight hush
a library dreams

in story and nocturne
secrets of the garden
before video veiled its stacks.

Now in Clio's archives
dilettantes and censors
rarely choose to whisper.

The smug and Tory
color-blind to wonder
cut conservators of *Don Quixotes.*

Zealots choose
the future of the mouth
yet shun the *Dialogues*

which salvaged Socrates
that we might live the good
with words saved from the hemlock.

The Bible chained by mold
and *The Federalist* interred by dust
survive with spines not broken to copy

and Athenaeum will preserve
for tomorrow's avant-garde
the therapy of Austen's manners

easing imagination across
the border from *Inferno,*
heaven being a quiet library

where just a few years past
a pair of lovers hid in the stacks,
the air scented with novels.

The Atmospherics of Melancholy

The earth has clouded to pastels
and dampened gilt excitement

for drizzle mock the mood
that drips self-pity to despair:

now's time to scrub both varnish
and verdigris from fancy

highlighting subtle shades
not blent in blanching deserts

but awash, persist like Johnson
walking from Litchfield to London

soaking wet, knowing rain
has not discolored his choices.

Inamorata

Neat Ethyl with flat bosom
and drawn-out neck did hex
our shack-up as a twosome
to flop at real sex.

Her fanny flat in wrapper,
her cap on tiny head,
I languished for this flapper
but drooped when in her bed.

She lured me with her tresses
rinsed a dishwater blond,
I blacked-out from caresses
her bra spelled, "Bottled in Bond."

Now freed by real Ethel
with sober soul to laud,
we name our love-nest Bethel
for ladder-steps to God.

Cosmos Koan

I asked God
to work a miracle.

But God replied:
"This morning did you see
the sun rise in the west?"

First Draft

Heaven is blacked out
and boarded up with secrets
beneath quiescent slate.

On this side there's grit
fantasies of rainbows
and curiosity—

soon little owls will copy
what they see on those walls,
epiphanies in chalk.

Breaking the Cycle

The air droops with cicadas
so relentless their life seems
hummed from eternity. Yet I
can't remember seventeen years ago
in the circadian foam their crunching
underfoot, bobbing in the pool,
and blotching the trees with oval warts.

That liquid year I had drunk
underground, burying past, present,
and punctuation. Releasing
three years later from fey loam
livid with cicatrix liver
I see a tired metaphor-in-bond,
in gratitude sing somewhat off key.

We Athenians

Today we stand upon Acropolis
where Parthenon transcends a cloudless sky,
but we discount the Areopagus
a tiny mound whose neither size nor art
earns sanctuary for the goatish gods.
Here Paul absorbing Greek philosophy
stands up to Stoics who considered God
beyond interpretation as they write
graffiti *to an unknown deity.*

Though Socrates still questions ancient gods
and lighted caves to see the shadowed walls,
we fear to leave this hilltop of the dark,
a sated haven for us Epicures.

Like dancers decorate a Grecian urn
Athena's women carry bowls of fire
(chastising Paul for his misogyny)
whose incense floats across the firmament
where Socrates and Paul award new shrines
not to Acropolis and Parthenons,
but lecterns where we stand-up Skeptics pan
all superstitions, cults and horny gods,
yet like the dying Socrates still hedge
and pay the debt we owe Asclepius.

1935

Another year in which too many idle
daydream and say their ship will soon come in,
will come in out of the bottle and reward
their service in the war to end all wars,
a dubious faith as Father took a drink
and said America had never lost
a war. He might have added reverie
kept history from being more complex.

Just two years free from Prohibition's try
a better discipline than law arose:
my Father would not drink when he must beg,
and one dry drunk in Akron calls a surgeon
for he must help another drunk to stay
away from that first drink. And so it was
Bill Wilson never took another drink
and soon the surgeon, Doctor Bob, would stop,
be free along with millions where for all
of history no messenger had told
how abstinence and twelve short steps with God
could keep that phantom ship within the bottle.

My Father never took another drink,
perhaps he did not have that thirsty craving
from which other men were being freed
in meetings where a group of people prayed.

My Father went out walking with his God
and though I haven't seen him doing crosswords
since nineteen seventy-two, I hear him nightly:
"What seven-letter word spells paradise?"